Bear in the Bathtub

a collaborative story about bears—real and imaginary

Fictional Story by Kathleen Dent
Illustrations by Alli DePuy and students across the country
Non-fiction based on the research by Dr. Mike Sawaya

ISBN: 1985824957
ISBN-13: 978-1985824959

Dear Big People:

Those of us who spend time with our favorite little people know what a joy it is to see them discover the natural world. This book is meant to spark the light of curiosity in kids, so they can explore the amazing places, people and creatures roaming our earth. Encourage kids to use their imaginations, get outside, and find out what the wild world is all about! Be curious like Mia, her friends across the country who have shared their artwork, and Dr. Mike Sawaya who is so curious about nature he has spent his life studying bears and other critters.

Curiosity is the wick in the candle of learning.
William Arthur Ward

Mia was a curious, curious girl. She loved to sneak and snoop. She loved to hide and watch and wait. But most of all, Mia loved being outdoors in the big, beautiful world.

Mia and her family lived in a great spot to be curious. Their backyard was a forest full of tall, tall trees, velvety green logs, bright flowers and all kinds

Everyday, after breakfast, Mia would slam out the back door, yell, "Bye, Mom! I'm going for an explore in the woods!" Her Mom would always yell back, "Have a good explore, Mia but don't forget to come home for dinner and your bath!

Mia never wanted to come back inside--even for dinner and ESPECIALLY-- not for a bath. There was just too much tromping, and tramping, and sneaking, and snooping to do in the deep, dark woods.

Monday was Mud Pie Day. Mia tromped down to the boggy bog next to the creek. She spent all day building her Mud Pie Bakery. She decorated Mud Cakes with pine cones, buttercups, sedges, and grass. She also built a hotel for the worms that wriggled through her fingers.

Mia dragged herself home finally and had some dinner. Her Mom looked at her mud caked hair and laughed, "Oh! It must have been Mud Pie Monday! Go upstairs for your bath!"

Mia sighed and clomped up the stairs. She opened the door to the bathroom and quickly shut it. "Mom!" Mia yelled. "I can't take a bath!
There's a bear in the bathtub!"

"Oh, Mia! Don't be ridiculous. The bears are all in the forest! What would a bear be doing in the bathtub?" her Mom replied.

Mia didn't take a bath on Monday!

Tuesday was Hide and Watch Day. Mia hid in the tall bushes next to the creek. She watched with her binoculars as the osprey parents hunted. Diving from high up in the sky to splash in the water and catch a wriggly trout in their talons.

Tuesday night when Mia's mom said, "Take your bath, Mia" She said, "Okay, I'm going to catch fish in the bathtub, just like the osprey!" Mia's mom smiled.

But when Mia opened the bathroom door, OH NO! "Mom!" Mia squealed--I can't be an osprey because THERE's A BEAR IN THE BATHTUB!"

"Mia! I told you the bears are out in the forest. There isn't one in our bathtub!" "Oh yes there is! And you won't believe what he is doing!"

Mia didn't take a bath on Tuesday.

Wednesday was Skitter Scatter Day. Squirrels and chipmunks and mice and rabbits skittered and scattered through the woods. Mia loved following their tracks over logs and rocks. She peeked into their holes and spied their cache of nuts and mushrooms.

When Mia got home from skittering and scattering all day her hair was full of twigs and her knees were stained mossy green. "Mia, you DEFINITELY need to take a bath tonight." "Okay, Mom," Mia moaned "I will if there isn't a bear in the bathtub." Her Mom just gave Mia 'Mom Eyes'.

So, Mia went upstairs. Bubbles were floating down the hallway. "Yikes! MOM! There is a **BEAR** again and this time he has bubble bath!"

"Oh really, Mia? Does he have a rubber ducky too?" "YUP! Mia yelled back "And more!" Mia's mom just sighed...

Mia didn't take a bath on Wednesday.

Thursday was Camouflage Day. Mia collected scraps of fabric, beads, old jewelry, and treasures. She followed her favorite trail observing the blue lupine, red Indian paintbrush, and the hot pink fireweed. Mia saw the black and grey nuthatch with the white belly and the shiny blackbirds with bright red wing patches. She saw the beautiful orange and black monarch butterflies and fancy designs on the swallowtail.

Then she took her treasures and made costumes for herself to match the flowers and the birds and the butterflies.

Mia was so tired at the end of the day that when her Mom said, "Mia!" and pointed upstairs to the bathroom, she didn't even complain. A nice hot bath sounded good! But when she opened the bathroom door.... there was that BEAR lounging in the water, taking his own sweet time! MOM! He is there again shampooing his hair!" "Oh, Mia! Don't say ONE MORE WORD! I've had enough! Bears are in the forest! Off to bed with you!"

Mia didn't take a bath on Thursday!

Friday was Mia's favorite day of all in the forest. Friday was Fort Day. As Mia explored in the forest every day, she noticed the homes that the animals made. The osprey had their nest way up in the top of a tree. The squirrel's black eyes gleamed out of a hole in the tree trunk. The deer had soft, grassy beds under the shady bushes, and even the bears had a winter time den far back in the woods.

Mia spent Fridays building her own little fort out of sticks and fir boughs and moss. Sometimes she would even build furniture out of logs and rocks and invite her stuffed animals for special tea parties in the glade.

Mia left her Friday Fort and wandered through the forest toward home for dinner. She hoped she could take a bath tonight because she was really starting to smell, and her head was all itchy so when her mom said, "Mia, you ABSOLUTELY, POSITIVELY MUST take a bath tonight!" Mia looked up at her with tears in her eyes and said, "Will you PLEASE come upstairs and get the bear out of the bathtub, so I can?" Mia's mom shook her head, grabbed Mia's hand and went up the stairs.

When Mia's Mom pushed open the door, she SCREAMED! "MIA THERE IS A BEAR IN THE BATHTUB!"

"I know Mom," Mia said quietly. "That's what I've been trying to tell you. And he's used up all the soap!"

Are you curious about bears and wonder if they ever go in bathtubs? Let Dr. Mike Sawaya tell you about what he has learned about REAL bears in the forest.

Why is the Bear in the Bathtub?

An explanation by Dr. Mike Sawaya, who studies creatures for a living.

So why is the bear in the bathtub? Simply put, when it's hot outside, bears take "baths" to cool down. To survive, animals keep their body temperatures the same even when outside temperatures change; this process is called *thermoregulation*.

Warm-blooded species such as the American black bear (Ursus americanus) have a hard time regulating body temperatures because they have large bodies, non-working sweat glands, and thick coats of dark fur that absorb the sun's rays. These traits make it a real challenge for black bears to cool down on hot days.

In northern climates, such as Montana, bears need lots of food reserves (i.e. fat) to survive through 5-6 months of winter hibernation. Fat is an efficient way to store calories, but it also insulates so more fat means a larger, hotter body.

In the fall, bears go through a period of increased activity known as *hyperphagia* (excessive hunger) to prepare for *hibernation*. During this time bears can consume up to 20,000 calories per day; this would be like eating 7 whole pizzas, 40 cheeseburgers or 133 candy bars in a single day!

The same layer of fat that helps bears to survive harsh winters can make bears hot in late summer and early fall. Although outside air temperatures are often highest in June and July, bears take the most baths in August and September when air temperatures are high and fat layers are thick.

During hyperphagia, bears need to keep eating even when it's hot and they don't want to move or be out in the sun. Natural and artificial water sources may allow bears to cool their core body temperatures down quickly and return to feeding rather than waste valuable berry-eating time sitting under a shady tree.

Why does this matter?

Our climate is changing, and the world is heating up! The number of hot days during hyperphagia will continue to increase with climate change, which means bears WANT to be inactive, but NEED to be active to meet their food requirements. Recent news reports indicate that bears may be spending more and more time in backyard swimming pools beating the heat.

This behavior may bring more bears into contact with people and that could lead to more conflicts with the possibility of someone getting hurt. In June 2018, a new science project was started in Yellowstone National Park to understand why and how bears use water sources for thermoregulation and this information will help wildlife managers make better decisions for public safety and bear conservation.

About this book...

This book is a collaborative effort. That is the way the <u>best</u> learning happens.

Dr. Mike Sawaya got us interested in his study about Yellowstone's bears and their use of stock tanks and ponds to cool off in the summer.

So we asked students from across the country to imagine what a bear would be doing in the bathtub? Their artwork brings the book to life.

We had a great time writing the story and illustrating Mia's adventures hoping to inspire kids to be curious about their world.

Thanks to all—and the bears—for this collaboration.

Alli Depuy and Kathleen Dent
Inspired Classroom
www.inspiredclassroom.com

Dr. Michael Allen Sawaya, Ph.D. has been studying carnivore populations in the United States and Canada for the past 20 years. Mike is a carnivore ecologist with Sinopah Wildlife Research Associates in Missoula, MT and his current studies include black bear thermoregulation at water sources, river otter genomics, cougar and black bear population dynamics in Yellowstone, and the effects of environmental change on wolverine demography and genetics in western North America. When Mike is not wrangling bear hair or following cougar tracks in snow, he enjoys camping, hiking, skiing, gardening, and traveling with his wife and two sons.

Alli DePuy and Kathleen Dent are the owners of Inspired Classroom in Missoula, Montana. Both Alli and Kathleen are educators and 'edupreneurs' creating innovative, collaborative learning experiences that bring the world into the classroom. Both enjoy tromping through the wild with the big and little people in their lives.